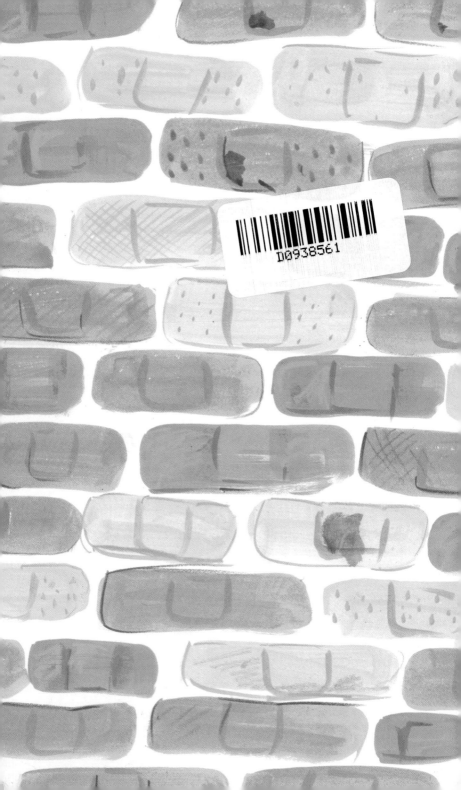

D0938561

BOX of PAIN PRESENTS:

Douglas Coupland
+
Graham Roumieu

HIGHLY INAPPROPRIATE TALES FOR YOUNG PEOPLE

Random House Canada

PUBLISHED BY RANDOM HOUSE CANADA

Copyright © 2011 Douglas Coupland
Illustrations © 2011 Graham Roumieu

Published in 2011 by Random House Canada, a division of Random House of Canada Limited, Toronto, and simultaneously in the United Kingdom by William Heinemann, a division of The Random House Group, Ltd., London. Distributed in Canada by Random House of Canada Limited.

www.randomhouse.ca

LIBRARY AND ARCHIVES CANADA CATALOGUING IN PUBLICATION

Coupland, Douglas
Highly inappropriate tales for young people / Douglas Coupland ; illustrations by
Graham Roumieu.

Issued also in electronic format.

ISBN 978-0-307-36066-3

I. Roumieu, Graham II. Title.

PS8555.O8253H54 2011   C813'.54   C2011-901903-5

PRINTED AND BOUND IN CANADA

2 4 6 8 9 7 5 3 1

This Box Contains:

Fruit Juice }

Evil }

Added
Sugar }

Donald,
the Incredibly Hostile Juice Box

Donald was a juice box with a terrible attitude. Out of nowhere, he'd whale on the other juice boxes, slamming them with plastic lunchroom trays and puncturing their sacred tinfoil puncture holes with bobby pins he swiped from the girls who sat at the popular girls' table.

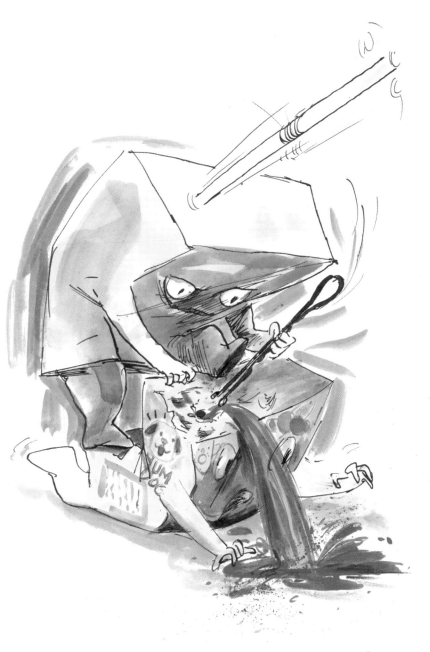

After lunch hour, when the cafeteria staff held respectful farewell ceremonies for all the juice boxes that had donated their nectar to the student body that day, Donald would run around the kitchen looking for things to throw into the deep fryer. This was annoying, but also kind of amusing—like when he dropped an entire lost and found drawer full of cellphones and dental retainers into the melted lard left over from Catfish Friday.

That actually made him a bit of a hero to the lunch ladies and the teachers, but Janitor Schwinn had to cancel his line dancing class that evening to stay late to drain the deep fryer and scrape melted iPods from its bottom. As far as Janitor Schwinn was concerned, Donald should have been buried in the recycling bins months back. But in the end, it took a truly fiendish deed to get Donald expelled from the school.

6

You see, Donald was obsessed with getting other juice boxes squished beneath the wheels of cars coming out of the teachers' parking lot. It's obviously amusing to see things get squished, but Donald carried it too far. There was something about watching hundreds of pounds of pressure from a moving vehicle blow out the bottoms of his fellow juice boxes that made Donald crazy—crazy for *destruction*.

He'd lure his juice box targets out to the teachers' parking lot by telling them lies. For example, he told one box that he'd heard of a new type of drinking straw that allows a person to drink without puncturing the foil hole on the top. It was a silly lie, but juice boxes are pretty stupid, and luring them to the scene of their deaths was never difficult.

Once Donald had snagged a box, he'd position his victim on the south side of the big speed bump where the teachers' lot exits onto the main road. He told each victim that if he waited there, he'd be right back with an example of the Magic Straw, or whatever it was he'd promised that time. So, while the juice box was waiting for a non-existent straw, Donald would hop up onto a traffic cone and do something to distract the teachers driving out of the lot. Sometimes he'd throw pebbles at the cars; sometimes he'd throw little metal stars made by the guys in shop class who smoked out behind the asbestos storage bins. If there weren't an innocent juice box about to meet a fiendish and horrible death by squishing, Donald's behaviour would be funny. But their imminent murder gave the scenario a bad taste: a taste of *evil*.

One day after math class, Donald was walking around removing chewing gum from beneath chairs and putting it up on the seats when he overheard the math teacher, Miss Burnside, on her cellphone screaming at someone from an online dating website. Something had to be wrong with their service, she said, because she hadn't had a nibble in months, and she wanted her money back. From there, she went on a rant about her life in general. Talked about the scary dates she'd had over the years, with one train wreck after another. Then she lashed into her students,

saying how cow-like and stupid they were, and that there was no point teaching them math because they could barely speak, let alone do long division. She wanted out of her life, but didn't know how to do it.

That was when Miss Burnside saw Donald, hiding behind a trash can. She went running after him, but it was too late: Donald had seen her true self, and she knew that soon he would begin to torment her.

Later that same afternoon, when Miss Burnside was
driving her car out of the teachers' parking lot, Donald
placed a victim juice box by the speed bump of doom.
When Miss Burnside's car approached, he hopped up onto
a traffic pylon and did something more extreme than usual.

Miss Burnside shrieked. The menthol cigarette she
was smoking dropped onto her lap and then rolled beneath
the seat. Startled, she hit the gas, and the car lurched
forward. She collected her wits, braked to a stop then got
out of the car, only to see that the doomed juice box had
shot out its guts in a massive, fruit-flavoured explosion.

Donald danced with happiness atop his pylon.

15

The next day when Donald showed up at school, he was met at the door by Principal Reeve, Janitor Schwinn and Miss Burnside. They told him he was a horrible little juice box, that his attitude stank, and that he was no longer welcome at the school. Both Janitor Schwinn and Miss Burnside wore gloating smiles that made Donald angry. He turned and walked away, but when classes began, he went to the parking lot, jimmied open Miss Burnside's and Janitor Schwinn's gas caps and stuffed their gas lines with dirt and litter before putting the caps back on. He thought, That'll teach them not to mess with my life! And, sure enough, their cars never worked, ever again.

Donald then went off in search of a new school at which to inflict mayhem. Walking down the roads and highways of the city, he resembled litter, so nobody paid him any attention except for the fast-food trash he passed along the way, who taunted him: "You're only a lowly juice box. You'll never be a carton. You'll never be a can. You're just a dumb little juice box that nobody cares about."

That did it. Donald used a piece of broken pop bottle as a magnifying lens and set fire to the fast-food trash that had been sassing him. With a demented cackle, he walked away as the trash burned. Then he burst into a military marching song:

I'm a juice box, I've been told.

Doom and mayhem good as gold.

Don't you ever mess with me.

I will steep your bones for tea.

1. 2. 3. 4.

Juice box guts are on the floor.

5. 6. 7. 8.

Death and I are on a date.

Sandra,

the Truly Dreadful Babysitter

Sandra was a truly dreadful babysitter. On her first job, her boss Peggy at the agency sent Sandra to babysit a pair of twins, Jason and Kaylee, whose parents were off to a high school reunion.

Sandra arrived at sundown, and asked the twins what they wanted to do. They said they wanted to play video games and text their friends, and Sandra said, "Those are stupid and boring ideas. Let's all go shoplifting."

"Shoplifting? We can't go shoplifting!"

"Nonsense. Get your sweaters."

The children thought Sandra was joking, and they decided to humour their babysitter. So the trio walked to the dollar store at the local mall, where Sandra said to Jason, "Prove to me you're brave and go steal a badminton set for me."

Jason was shocked. "But I don't want to!"

Sandra looked at him. "Jason, you may just be too dumb and useless to steal. But if you don't, I won't like you anymore."

Jason had been raised to try to see the good in people, and so, against his better judgment, he went into the store to shoplift a badminton set.

Sandra then said to Kaylee, "Now it's your turn. Go in and steal me a hair dryer."

"Why do you want a hair dryer?"

Sandra grew fierce. "Kaylee, I want my hair dryer and I want it *now*."

Kaylee started crying, but Sandra shoved her into the store. "Stop snivelling. I'm sick of children who don't have any guts."

While her charges were in the store, Sandra stared at the sidewalk and found a half-smoked cigarette stubbed out on the concrete. "Beautiful. I'll paint my lungs with smoke," she said.

Lighting up, Sandra peered in the window at the store's owner behind the cash—a morbidly obese man named Raymond, who'd just had a huge fight with his wife because she'd lost all of their savings buying lottery tickets. Bulky and miserable, Raymond had his eagle eyes on the twins, and as they made their way to the front door, he grabbed them both by their ears and dragged them into the back room.

The door slammed behind them, but even from out on the sidewalk, Sandra could hear the children's screams and protests that their shoplifting binge wasn't their fault. Sandra also heard slapping and crunching sounds and thought, *Great, there goes my new badminton set and my hair dryer.* She walked home.

29

The next day the phone rang. When Sandra picked it
up, Peggy said, "Really, Sandra, you can't take your
charges shoplifting and then abandon them when they
get caught."

"I suppose you're right, but they were such snivellers."

"Okay, but I hope you've learned your lesson. Sandra,
I see something special in you—something fresh and
new—so I think you deserve another chance. Here's the
address of your next charge, young Hunter, who I'm sure is

a total cream puff to babysit." Young Hunter's parents were
going out for a Thai dinner and then to see a retrospective
of the films of Russell Crowe.

When Sandra asked Hunter what he'd like to do,
Hunter said he'd like to take some wieners and some
of that dough that comes in a can and make piggies in
a blanket.

"That's a stupid idea," Sandra said. "Why don't we take cardboard boxes, draw doors and windows on them, pretend they're hotels and office buildings and set fire to them."

Hunter said, "I'm afraid of fire."

"Afraid of fire?" said Sandra, appalled. "Hunter, hasn't surfing the Internet toughened you up at all? How do you expect me to like someone so feeble and frightened? Come on. Help me find some boxes."

Hunter had been trained to be polite to his elders and agreed against his instincts.

So Hunter and Sandra found a bunch of boxes, and as they used Sharpies to draw doors, windows and signage on the boxes, Hunter even began to have fun. "Look," said Hunter. "This is a hotel for people who can't walk."

Sandra looked at his box. "Cross out the doors so that there's no possibility of escape."

"Okay." Hunter scribbled out the doors cheerfully. "This is highly amusing," he said.

Sandra, in the meantime, had created a city block of pretend buildings. "The real fun starts now, Hunter," she said. "Help me pile all these boxes in the fireplace."

Sandra and Hunter stuffed the fireplace full.

When Hunter looked at Sandra dubiously, she said, "Not to worry. This fireplace can easily handle all of this." She handed him a small box of wooden matches. "Go ahead."

"Are you sure, Sandra?"

"Just *do* it!"

So Hunter set fire to the hotel for people who can't walk, and to the saltine cracker box that was a prison for shoplifters, and to the Prada shoebox that had become a shelter for lost puppies.

Fwoomp!!!!!

All the boxes went up in flames, and the wall above the fireplace caught fire, too, and soon the whole room was ablaze.

Sandra said, "Hunter, I think we should leave."

Hunter, staring horrified at the flames, burst into tears.

"Oh, be quiet," Sandra told him. "*You're* the one who lit the match. It was all your fault, Hunter. *Everything.*"

She led the sobbing boy out onto the sidewalk, and when the fire trucks arrived, she headed home.

"Sandra, I know babysitting is not the best job on earth," Peggy said on the phone the next morning. "But please, don't set fire to peoples' houses."

"*He* lit the match, not me."

S andra's next assignment was to take care of a young
girl named Brenlinn, whose parents were using a
downloaded discount coupon to feast at an all-you-can-eat
prawn restaurant.

After the parents were safely out the door, Sandra
leaned down to the little girl and asked, "Brenlinn, what
would you like to do?"

"Maybe watch TV?" she replied.

"That is *so* unimaginative, Brenlinn."

"What do you want to do then?"

"I want to go for a healthy walk in the night air. You
watch far too much TV, and your body needs some
exercise."

"I hate walking!" whined Brenlinn.

"Tough," said Sandra. "I'm in charge and we're going for
a walk. *Now!*"

The two entered the cemetery grounds, Sandra holding up her cellphone to light up what little path there was. As they walked deep, deep into the cemetery's interior, the little girl shied from every shadow.

Suddenly the cellphone rang, and Sandra looked at its screen. She said to Brenlinn, "It's Todd, this guy who's really into me. I have to take it." She held the phone up to her ear eagerly. "Todd? Are you there? Hi! It's Sandra—"

But then the phone's battery died and Sandra was furious. "Great. Todd finally calls and I've wasted all my battery power to make a flashlight to guide *you*."

"Sandra?" It was pitch black, so dark Brenlinn couldn't see anything. "Sandra?" she squeaked again.

But Sandra had already gone. Her innate sense of direction guided her back to the road, and she walked home, eager to recharge her battery and put the night behind her. As she opened the door to her house, a massive rainstorm began, and it lasted all night.

S andra was a truly dreadful babysitter. Brenlinn caught
pneumonia in the cemetery and nearly died. When
Peggy called Sandra to tell her this, Sandra said, "Peggy,
Brenlinn was a whiner. Honestly, the world would be much
better off without her."

"Oh, Sandra," said Peggy. "You're such a naughty little scamp. I'll phone you later today with your next baby-sitting assignment."

Just then, Sandra's cell beeped—it was Todd. "Gotta go, Peggy." She hung up and, when Todd came on, she told him all about her job babysitting horrible young children. "I love babysitting, Todd, but it can be really difficult when you have children who just won't behave."

End!

Hans,

the Weird Exchange Student

Hans was an exchange student, so nobody wanted anything to do with him. Everyone thought he was from one of those Eastern European countries with hard-to-remember names containing too few vowels—those countries where children are forced to wear corrective footwear and are only allowed to use medicine balls during gym class.

Hans was sort of okay at sports, and he wasn't freakishly odd, but he never really seemed to fit into his North American school, nor did he care to do so. He had no appreciation of the school's food chain. When he went to sit down with the Camera Club or the semi-popular girls, he created fear and confusion.

"It's the exchange student."

"Oh my god. He's coming towards our table."

"Run!"

So Hans was a little lonely, but at least he had the Internet to keep him company, and after a few months, his presence became invisible and forgotten as everyone learned to completely ignore him.

And then one day, Mindy from the cheerleaders' table noticed that instead of tossing his trash in the garbage can after lunch, Hans saved the remains of his lunch in a paper bag—and not only that, he actually took bits of *other peoples'* uneaten food and put it in his bag, too.

"Ashley, look. There—he's doing it right now."

"What a freak! Where does he come from?"

"One of those countries where you buy your wife online."

"Ick."

"Look, he just put half an egg sandwich in his bag!"

Soon the two cheerleaders were fascinated with watching Hans sneak food remains, and when he left the cafeteria, they decided to follow him.

Hans walked past the baseball field and the dugouts where the kids on the failure track smoked cigarettes and swapped tips on how to get hired vacuuming interiors at the local car wash. Then he walked past the chop shop where stolen cars were taken apart to be shipped to Russia, and after that he crossed the dirt road pancaked with flattened small animals. Finally, he walked past the water reservoir tank in the unmown grasslands that swept out to the highway.

"This is such a good place to bury a body," said Mindy to Ashley, as they walked a safe distance behind Hans.

"I agree," said Ashley. "You can almost feel all the corpses of murdered nurses and hitchhikers under our feet."

"What's he doing?" Mindy exclaimed.

Hans was carefully unloading his bag of uneaten food onto the ground, arranging it into different piles: sandwiches, snack cakes, pudding and pudding type products and so forth. Then he started on the sandwich pile, separating luncheon meat in one pile, soggy bread in another.

Mindy whispered, "Maybe it's a religious thing."

"Maybe he's into ecology," Ashley said.

"Do you think he's murdered anybody?"

"Don't start a rumour yet, Mindy. Not until we see more of what he's capable of."

"Now he's repackaging all of the food groups!"

"Weird!"

Hans put the luncheon meats and meat-like products into a clear plastic zip-lock bag, bread into a paper bag. Each food category got its own bag.

Then Hans gathered all of these bags inside the original big lunch bag and placed it in the centre of the clearing, laying a single french fry on top.

Mindy and Ashley burst out from their grassy hiding spot.

"Okay, there, Exchange Student Guy, we're onto you. We know you're doing something weird here."

Hans was perplexed. "I am doing nothing wrong."

"Don't be cute with us. You're doing something unusual. We don't even know what to call it, whatever it is you're doing."

Hans said, "I am playing an enjoyable game of *Karkassetasche*."

"What on earth did you just say?"

"*Karkassetasche*. It's a German word."

"We thought you were from one of those new countries where you buy your wife online."

Hans laughed. "No, I am from Germany. You still have to find a wife the old-fashioned way there."

Ashley asked, "Are you from the rich Germany or the poor Germany?"

"Alas, I am from the former East Germany, although I have only ever known a unified Germany in my lifetime."

"Why did you put all of the food in separate bags inside a bigger bag?"

"Ahhh . . . because of *Karkassetasche*, the game I invented."

"Does it involve murder or Hitler or anything?"

"No. It only involves *die Krähen*."

"Dee *what?*"

"*Die Krähen*—crows." Hans pointed to a dozen crows sitting on the rim of the water reservoir tank. "Crows have an insatiable blood lust. I find it admirable: *Blutrausch*."

"You're being too German for us," said Mindy. "What's this about crows and blood?"

"Ah. You see, a crow will almost never kill another animal, but if it finds one that is already dead, it will gorge on its flesh, ripping out its internal organs in a spray of hunger and blood."

Ashley looked at Hans. "Crows sure are interesting."

"They are indeed . . . what is your name?"

Ashley blushed. "I'm Ashley."

"Well, Ashley, my name is Hans. I find that if one wishes to have food re-enter nature, as opposed to simply putting it into a landfill, it is important to—"

"Stop," said Mindy. "Hans, you mean you're green and you put your green way of being into actual practice in your everyday life?"

"I try to."

"That is so adorable!" she exclaimed.

Hans said, "I like to make sure crows are able to feast upon cafeteria leftovers. Hence, *Karkassetasche*."

"What does that mean exactly?"

"It means 'carcass bag.' 'Carcass' + 'bag.' I tap into the crows' natural desire to rip apart carcasses. Were I to place food on the ground without the appropriate packaging, the crows would probably leave it."

"I would never have thought of that," said Ashley, twirling her hair around a finger.

Hans looked at the bag on the ground and moved the lone french fry on top slightly to the side.

Ashley asked, "Okay, why the french fry?"

"That is what I call the *Auslöserkartoffel*—the trigger potato. It alerts the alpha crow to the presence of rich, nourishing carrion within the bag."

"You're so thoughtful," said Ashley. "Let's watch the crows rip apart the bag."

"An excellent idea," said Hans. "If we hide, they will become suspicious, but if we stand over there and pretend not to notice them, they will fly in, like vampires from the moon, to satisfy their deepest need for dead flesh."

Ashley elbowed Mindy in the ribs. "He's so *poetic!*"

They moved to the edge of the clearing, and Hans said, "What shall we pretend to talk about?"

"Don't worry about that, Hans—we never talk about anything, really," Ashley reassured him.

"Look!" said Mindy. "The crows are coming!"

58

And indeed, the crows were swooping down from the reservoir. The alpha crow cautiously approached the carcass bag and then ripped a huge gash across its belly, allowing its contents to spill onto the soil. Within seconds, all the crows were at it, ripping and tearing, gleefully and methodically gorging on its sweet, succulent contents.

"They're like my grandparents at the casino!" said Ashley.

Hans, meanwhile, watched the trash hysteria with a sense of fatherly pride. "I am glad to make the world a better place."

Ashley looked at him, her eyes aglow. "I'm sorry you're unpopular, Hans. But from now on, I'll be your girlfriend and you'll never have to worry about your popularity ever again." And she kissed the now popular Hans as mayonnaise and ketchup flecks flew through the air, at which point Hans bit her on the neck. This surprised her, but in a good way. "Hans! You mean you're a vampire on top of everything else?"

"Indeed I am."

It was one of life's perfect moments.

Brandon,
the Action Figure With Issues

Brandon kept to himself after he returned from his tour of duty. His girlfriend had moved on with some guy who worked in a discount golf supply store, and when he spoke with her, in a half-hearted attempt to get her back, it felt like she wasn't even a human being any more. Nobody seemed real any more—the people from his old life were walking ghosts he couldn't connect with.

Brandon found it easier to live by himself with his personal necessities stored and ready for action in a Japan Airlines business-class toiletry bag he'd found in the trash. That way he could be nimble if the situation changed wherever he was sleeping, which was mostly behind the juniper hedge at the public library, where the crows couldn't get at him and rip away at his rarely washed fatigues.

The library front desk let him use the bathroom in exchange for guarding the property from graffiti taggers. For money, Brandon foraged around under the seats of unlocked cars while their owners were in the library. He used the money to buy white bread and Campbell's soup, which he ate straight from the can using his lucky spoon. His Friday afternoon treat was a stick of gum from that cute gal who worked at the Goodwill store, who seemed as if she kind of liked him, except she was obviously CIA, so no go.

The winter had so far been mild, and Brandon thought he could continue with his highly mobile lifestyle indefinitely, never having to engage with human beings again. Then disaster struck in the form of a monster named Cooper.

Cooper stayed in his mother's SUV while she ran into the building to look for books about TED conferences. Cooper had tried to set his mother straight: "You're being totally clueless, because the whole point of TED conferences is that they're online and not books at all."

"Cooper, I'm too young to be just your mother and nothing else. I need something to feed my mind."

"Well, you're not going to find what you're looking for. You might as well try to look for TED slide shows as to look for TED books."

After Cooper's mother went into the library, the boy searched the parking lot for something to occupy his enormous energy. He spotted Brandon behind the junipers, and he got out of the vehicle and went over for a closer look. Brandon would normally have been out of there like a shot, but he was having the sweats, a recurring condition he blamed on his mandatory anthrax vaccination back in '08.

Cooper grabbed Brandon. "Gotcha!"

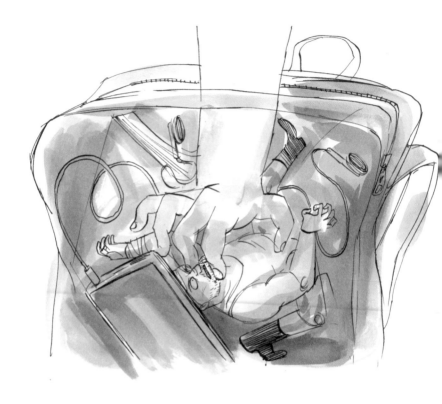

Before Brandon could react, Cooper had stuffed him
into his school backpack and climbed into the car. When
Cooper's mother came back a minute later—carrying no
TED books, as Cooper had predicted—Brandon's angry
protests were muffled by the backpack's nylon fabric.
Cooper's mom assumed it was just music noise coming
from the buds on Cooper's iPhone.

At home, Cooper went to his room on the third floor
and took Brandon from his backpack and stuck him in a
long vacant gerbil cage. "You need to dry out, Sarge."

After Cooper left, Brandon stood in the gerbil cage, wondering if what just happened really had happened. He briefly shook the tiny bars. Then he went to get some bread from his vinyl bag—which was when he realized it was still lying behind the hedge, where raccoons or drifters or small birds would soon loot it. He fell into deeper despair and paced amid the cage's wood chips, which had a weird stench of powdered scrambled eggs and depleted uranium. The water bottle was empty. Brandon felt like it might be time to have the total inner collapse he'd been fearing ever since he saw two choppers collide over the munitions dump, causing a huge explosion, when he was stuck in a conked-out Jeep downwind and had to suck the whole mess into his lungs.

But Brandon tapped inner reserves honed by his service career and his life of homelessness by choice. The hamster wheel gave him a chance to burn off some adrenaline and focus on what would come next. Running at full blast, he made an inventory of everything in Cooper's room and began to plan.

Brandon may have had issues, but he remembered that boys like to play rough with their action figures. He could handle rough as well as anyone else, but kidnapping, imprisonment and no drinking water? *Vengeance, thy name is honey-sweet death.* Stoked from his run, fuelled by rage and energized by not taking his daily medication on time, Brandon bent the gerbil cage's bars and crawled out. He was free.

From his past, Brandon knew how action figure enthusiasts think and what they love to do. His first target was Cooper's chest of drawers. Beneath a mound of tube socks he hit pay dirt: a stash of twenty-four Mexican-made Halloween-grade M-80 cherry bombs with three-gram payloads. *¡Caramba!*

He bundled the explosives together with rubber bands and then crawled up the bookcase beside the door and made his HQ. There he assembled a cache including, among other things, a pillowcase, some string, a roll of duct tape and an unopened bottle of Polo cologne, an age-inappropriate gift from Cooper's grandmother.

Yes.

Then he lay in wait for the boy to return from laser paintball. To Brandon it felt like waiting for Christmas morning.

He heard the sound of feet on the stairs, then Cooper was yelling, "Fine! Go to your stupid serenity workshop! And take your reheatable shepherd's pie with you. I'm sick of Whole Foods deli stuff, anyway. I'll make myself some Kraft dinner!"

The downstairs front door slammed shut and Cooper came into his room, muttering, "Stupid mother, stupid—"

Pounce!

Before Cooper could turn the lights on, Brandon had parachuted onto Cooper's head with the pillowcase. Retrieving the duct tape slung over his shoulder, he quickly taped the pillowcase shut at the neck, screaming, "I didn't go to war to fight for you, you parasite. You don't deserve your freedom!"

Cooper was hopping around, screaming, "Get off me! What the heck do you think you're doing?"

Zzzzzzzzzzzzzip!

A long strip of tape at mouth level muffled Cooper, but he continued to hop around, trying to scrape Brandon off his shoulders. With a tight grip on the edge of the pillowcase, Brandon rode Cooper like a buckaroo.

Then he emptied the full bottle of cologne onto Cooper's head. "Smell that, buddy? Smells like *freedom*, doesn't it!"

Brandon leaped to the floor and lassoed Cooper's ankles together, causing him to trip face first onto the carpet. While he remained dazed, Brandon lashed Cooper's hands together. Down came the M-80s, whose fuses he lit with a short-circuited wire ripped out of a lamp.

The twenty-four mini-bombs went off beside Cooper's head as Brandon barked, "Who owns who, huh? *Who?*" He ripped the tape off, but Cooper said nothing. In a burst of heat and light and smoke, the last of the M-80s went off.

Brandon screamed, "Who. Owns. *You?*"

"You do."

"I can't hear you."

"You own me."

"Say it properly!"

"*Sir,* you own me, *sir.*"

Brandon cut off a lock of Cooper's hair. "This is what's known in the freedom business as a trophy."

He then cut Cooper loose and walked out the door.

"All any of us want in life is freedom, son. You have a fine night." With that, Brandon was gone.

Cooper said, "Man, that guy has issues."

Cindy,

the Terrible Role Model

Cindy had been a child star who experienced way too much way too early in life—money, fame, designer endorsements, fan mail from guys in jail—and she didn't handle any of it well. It didn't help that she also had terrible people around her who gave her bad advice and stole all the high-end items from her goodie bags at award shows, leaving behind the useless stuff like low-end lip balm, made-in-China key fobs and depressing medical research charity T-shirts. No one was surprised when, after a few years of this, Cindy came out of her fog of stardom to find that life had marooned her atop eleven-year-old Jennifer Gilroy's suburban bedroom desk at 3:45 on a Wednesday afternoon, astride a unicorn plush toy, scrutinizing her increasingly raisin-like vinyl in Jennifer's vanity mirror.

When Jennifer came home from school, she found Cindy on her unicorn on the desk. "Hi, Cindy. How was your day?"

"You look terrible," Cindy said. "You went to school dressed like that?"

"I thought I looked okay."

"Yeah, you do—assuming you want to scare guys away and don't care about having any friends. Did you get me my nicotine patches?"

"Yeah. But you should stop using them. Drugs are bad for you."

"I *would* end up getting stuck with Miss Goody Two-Shoes." Cindy hopped off the unicorn, jumped off the desk and walked out of Jennifer's bedroom, heading for the kitchen. "I hope your lush of a mother left some wine in the box."

"I had a great day, thank you, Cindy."

"Don' t be sarcastic with *me*, missy. It's not your style."

Jennifer followed Cindy to the kitchen. "My mom doesn't like it when you drink her wine," she said.

"Boo *hoo*. Listen to you, clomping your way around the place. You sound fat. Have you been gaining weight? Why do I even bother asking? Open the fridge door for me."

So Jennifer opened the door and Cindy hopped onto the fridge's second level with a Shania Twain 2002 World Tour collectible thimble. She held it under the wine box's spout and poured. She chugged one thimbleful and then poured another, which she drank more slowly.

Jennifer said, "Do you think you should chug it like that? You don't want to blow above 0.08 on the Breathalyzer."

"Don't throw math in my face. I hate math. It's hard, it's stupid, and it's nature's way of separating spinsters from women who end up breeding." She took another long sip.

"Cindy, how come you never had any kids?"

"You're asking me for real?"

"Yeah. I am."

"Fine, then I'll throw some math back at you: a woman's body needs seventeen to twenty-two percent body fat in order to be able to have kids. I've never been higher than ten. Happy now?"

"You could gain some weight."

"And wreck *this* body? What universe are you living in? Hey, is that onion dip I see on the shelf above me?"

"It is. Let me get it for you."

Soon the two were at the kitchen counter, Cindy using potato chip crumbs to scoop up the onion dip. "This stuff'll go straight to my hips, but it's nothing a quick puke can't undo. Jeez, Jennifer, your blackheads are like Play Doh Fun Factories squeezing out charcoal-coloured Play Doh."

Jennifer's shirt had come untucked, exposing pale white flesh. Cindy zeroed right in. "Would it kill you to visit a tanning bed?"

Jennifer reached into the cutlery drawer at the same time that she grabbed Cindy. With a pair of scissors, she quickly and efficiently cut the flailing former child star's signature sassy ponytail off at the crown and put Cindy back down on the counter.

Cindy stared at the tufts of her hair, which Jennifer had dropped onto the counter, and shrieked. "You crazy witch, what have you done!?" She ran over to the chrome-surfaced breadbox. "My ponytail! My long, beautiful signature hairstyle!"

"I've been wanting to cut it for weeks. Serves you right for never being supportive of anything I do, as well as fostering an unrealistic body image. Would it have killed you at least once to say that one of my outfits was flirty or fashion-forward?"

"You fat pig! I'm going to kill you!"

"You're six inches tall and made of plastic. Good luck."

Cindy put her tiny hands on her plastic hips. "Okay, then, you're on. See you in the cemetery."

Cindy hopped off the counter and ran into the living room, where she hid in the cold air vent, waiting for the right moment to kill Jennifer.

As she lurked in the chill aluminum tubing, Cindy recalled years ago hearing dark murmurings from people in the makeup and wardrobe departments about girls, and how they invariably cut off their Barbies' hair, put them in microwave ovens or Magic Markered them with tattoos before chucking them into the trash. Cindy had never believed that could be true. But today showed her . . . well, today showed her that in life, all the weird, scary things— those things that keep you awake at night—basically come true in the end, and genuinely ought to be feared.

Cindy also looked at her situation realistically. It's both hard and easy to kill a person if you're a doll. Being small gives you tactical advantages, but it also means you can't strangle a person with your bare hands, so one has to compensate by having a good, simple plan.

First she used a cellphone to hack into the house's intercom system and hectored Jennifer no matter where she went.

"Look at me. I'm Jennifer. I'm eleven years old and fat and have no friends and my family doesn't love me and soon I'm going to die. What's that, Bwana—an elephant approaching? No, it's merely that hideous carbohydrate dump named Jennifer."

Jennifer tried to talk back. "I'm going to be big about this, Cindy, and I'm going to forgive you for all these mean things you're saying."

"Be big about it? Honey, you already are big—big as this house."

Cindy decided that the most practical way to kill Jennifer would be to arrange for her to trip and fall down the staircase. Using the house's ductwork, she went from room to room, gathering the equipment she needed: fishing line, books, string and a knife.

At midnight, when Jennifer's parents were asleep, Cindy whispered on the intercom into Jennifer's bedroom, "I'm really sorry I've been so mean to you. I don't know what came over me. Maybe it was the wine and all the fat in the chip dip. It turned me into somebody else. You know I like you a lot. And I actually like my new short hair. It makes me feel like I just won another Emmy and I'm standing on the red carpet. Can we be friends again?"

Jennifer leaned down into her bedroom's heating duct and said, "I suppose so. Where are you?"

"I'll be right outside your door in a few seconds. Come out and we can have some fun flipping through magazines and making fun of peoples' outfits."

So Jennifer, who was a mostly peaceable person, opened the door and looked out. "Cindy?"

"Over here."

"Where?" she called, heading towards the stairs.

"Over here on the top step. I'd come to you, but I have cramps from the chip dip. I think it was past its expiry date."

"It was in the fridge a bit long. Next time, we'll . . ."

Whump!

A pile of books bound together with fishing line and tethered to a string moored on the hallway chandelier swung down and whacked Jennifer on the head, knocking her towards the stairs, where fishing line at ankle height finished the deed. Jennifer tumbled down, ending up in a mangled heap on the floor.

Since that day, Cindy, the terrible role model, has been on the run, one step ahead of the law, her only goal being to systematically eliminate girls like Jennifer who treat their dolls with disrespect. *They deserve it.*

Kevin,

the Hobo Minivan
with Extremely Low Morals

The thing about minivans is that they're usually pretty boring and stuffy. So when Kevin the minivan adopted the hobo lifestyle, it stuck out more than it would, say, were you or I to adopt the hobo lifestyle.

Kevin would feed daily with the other minivans, shortly after three in the afternoon, at local schoolyard parking lots. The minivans huddled in one patch of the lot while the SUVs huddled in another. Like most hobos, Kevin worked hard to stay just clean enough, and in just good enough shape so as not to be towed to the local impound lot, which, as all hobos know, is basically like being sentenced to death. Kevin was especially afraid of his arch-enemy, a tow truck named Darrell who had a skull and crossbones on his mud flaps. Kevin had made the mistake of honking at Darrell in traffic once.

So Kevin would lurk by himself somewhere in between the SUVs and minivans. His dining strategy was to look very boring and forgettable. He would sit there, his doors invitingly open, until a child, exhausted by a day of school, would say, "That minivan's for me."

Once the child climbed in, Kevin would slam the door shut and begin to shake as violently as a paint shaker at the hardware store until all of the spare change had been extracted from the pockets of the child. If he was extra lucky, he'd also score small electronic devices and the odd laptop that slipped out of a backpack.

Then Kevin would open his door, spit the child out and drive to the local Liquor Locker. He had an arrangement with Tony, the clerk, who would come into the parking lot with a plastic bag and accept Kevin's money and electronics. In return, Tony would pour forty ounces of cheap vodka into Kevin's gas tank, and Kevin was good to go for another day.

But as with most addictive things, his need for vodka increased, and Kevin had a bright idea. He put a sticker on his sliding door saying, THIS VEHICLE NOW HAS CARTOON OPTION. Within days, he'd doubled his vodka ration. Kevin may have been a hobo minivan, but he was proud of his hard work and good ideas.

Still, weekends were difficult for Kevin, as it was much harder to lure children inside for a shakedown. He tried hanging out at playgrounds and circuses, but he had trouble blending in with the crowd, so mostly he hung out at the local mall. But because it was the weekend, kids weren't burnt out from school and had more energy. They wouldn't fall for his ruse.

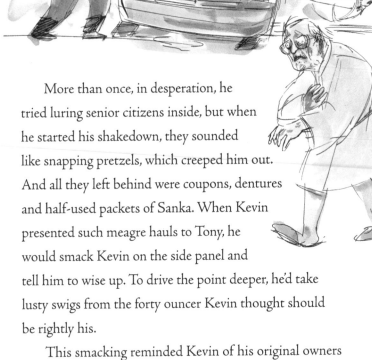

More than once, in desperation, he tried luring senior citizens inside, but when he started his shakedown, they sounded like snapping pretzels, which creeped him out. And all they left behind were coupons, dentures and half-used packets of Sanka. When Kevin presented such meagre hauls to Tony, he would smack Kevin on the side panel and tell him to wise up. To drive the point deeper, he'd take lusty swigs from the forty ouncer Kevin thought should be rightly his.

This smacking reminded Kevin of his original owners and how mean they were to him, dripping ice cream and barf all over his upholstery and driving him way too quickly up and down the freeway during custody weekends, making his tires sore. When Tony smacked Kevin, he felt awful and left an oil puddle on the Liquor Locker's concrete.

Though Kevin lived the hobo lifestyle to the fullest, he eventually grew tired of Tony's abuse and living in fear of tow trucks. He decided it was time to dream— and to make that dream come true! He would pull off the biggest shakedown ever and entrap an entire birthday party of rich, lazy and stupid children loaded down with cash and electronics. He'd take his haul to Tony one last time, who would fill him to the top with heavily advertised premium vodka, and then he'd drive to Florida, where his life would become a big, glamorous adventure. Goodbye to bad weather, mean-spirited SUVs and Tony's mood swings. Kevin was going to live.

He shared his dream with his fellow hobos at their nighttime encampment beneath the train bridge in the town's industrial section. They were highly supportive and encouraged Kevin to go for it. A pair of rusty shopping carts exclaimed, "We're too old to do that sort of thing, Kevin. You do it for *us*." Carl, the belligerent 1983 Chrysler K-car, emerged for a moment from his typical nightly pirate-like ranting and said, "*Arrr*, I'll never get out of this town alive, Kevin. But you . . . you're still young enough to get washed. You can still have your upholstery fumigated for bedbugs and have your rear-view mirrors reattached. My jig is up, Kevin, but all you have to do is say 'yes' to life."

And so Kevin decided to go for the gold. On a Saturday morning he asked Tony to scour Facebook for rich children's birthday parties in the vicinity, but Tony said he didn't need to go on Facebook. Rich people were always phoning him for liquor deliveries, and they told him a lot about their social lives.

Tony gave Kevin an address and helped prepare him for the mission. He washed Kevin's front window and then taped to his hood some half-deflated birthday balloons that had snagged in some tree branches at the edge of the parking lot.

When Kevin was ready, Tony said, "Okay, buddy—I've got fifty gallons of primo Grey Goose in the back loading dock waiting for you. Go and shake those rich brats something fierce."

The party was in a snappy part of town. Kevin was slightly intimidated by the absence of tow trucks and of people pushing around shopping carts full of discarded random objects. Where was the rich pageant of life? The sidewalks were free of people. All he saw were automated lawn sprinklers and well pruned trees whose branches contained no snagged white plastic shopping bags.

Kevin parked in the driveway of a posh home where young Amberly was celebrating her thirteenth birthday with a large crowd of friends. He opened his side door invitingly as his tailpipe sneezed with glee. On the door was a felt-penned sign he and Tony had cooked up:

AMBERLY'S SHUTTLE BUS
TO THE HIGH FASHION SHOW
LEAVING SHORTLY
FIFTY FREE TANNING BED HOURS
FOR THE FIRST TEN GUESTS

Sure enough, on her way into the party, Jenessa saw the sign and texted two friends to quickly and quietly come out to the van to go to the fashion show and score fifty free tanning bed hours. She texted, "I like Amberly but I like 50 free tanning hours better!" Jenessa's friends arrived and they, too, texted friends. Within minutes, the minivan was full of ten party guests.

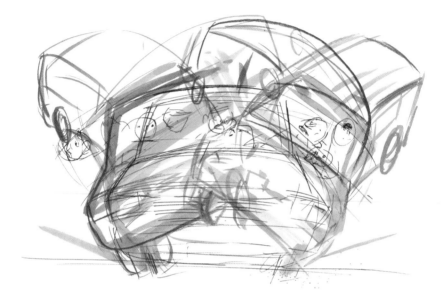

Kevin felt young, free and athletic for the first time in years, and he slammed his door shut and began to ferociously shake his load of teens. Coins, cellphones and gold jewellery began to fly around the minivan's interior. Kevin could already taste his Florida freedom.

That's when Kevin saw a big black tow truck come around the bend—his worst enemy, Darrell. Kevin quickly stopped shaking his passengers, opened his doors and coughed them out onto the sidewalk. He fled. Fortunately for him, Darrell was too preoccupied trying to learn the ins and outs of his new in dash navigation system, and he missed seeing the clump of sunbed worshippers as they landed in the flower bed by the roadside.

Back at the Liquor Locker, Tony said, "Let the treasure counting begin!" He flung open Kevin's doors and was shocked when he saw how little loot there was on the floor. "What happened?" Tony asked. "Did you shake them up or not?"

Kevin said, "Tony, I wasn't cut out for the good life. It was wrong for me to want something better for myself."

To this, Tony said, "Well, okay. I, too, learned long ago that it's really a lot easier in life if you have small, manageable dreams. Big dreams are for losers."

"Amen," sighed Kevin as Tony poured a bottle of discount vodka into his tank. "Dreaming leads to failure."

Mr. Fraser,

the Undead Substitute Teacher

Mr. Fraser looked like most substitute teachers, with the exception that he was a member of the walking dead. If you were to stab him with a sharp pencil, he wouldn't bleed. Instead, all he'd do was drip a bit of undead goo from the hole.

If the teachers in the staff room noticed that Mr. Fraser was a member of the walking dead, they never said anything, because subs were hard to come by. The female teachers had a secret agreement among themselves as to how to divvy out once-a-month spa days. Exposing Mr. Fraser as a walking corpse would have wrecked their system.

One morning Mr. Fraser showed up to cover for Miss Lincoln, who had told the principal she was going in for diabetes counselling, but who was actually across town getting an exfoliating moisture mask done with heated mitts to the sound of soothing New Age music. Her class quickly noted that Mr. Fraser's skin was as white as photocopy paper and that you could see his veins, as well as holes and gashes and bruises where he had injured himself, because members of the walking dead can't heal.

The class wasn't sure if Mr. Fraser was one of those substitute teachers who accept no guff from their students, or if he was one of those subs who love receiving ritual humiliation from their class. He just sort of sat there at his desk in his white short-sleeve dress shirt, not breathing.

One girl, Jane, raised her arm to ask if he was okay, but he snarled at her like a raccoon defending a piece of six-day-old Kentucky Fried Chicken, and didn't answer.

Everyone began texting.

IZ HE ALIVE?

I THINK HE MIGHT B DEAD.

HE'ZNT BREATHING.

I CAN C HIS ARTERIES

One student, William, got up to go to the bathroom, but Mr. Fraser roared, so William quickly sat down. Mr. Fraser picked up a piece of chalk and wrote on the board:

i'm Hungry

Shivers passed through the class of twenty.

Mr. Fraser sniffed the air and then grunted and picked up his desk like it weighed nothing and put it in front of the room's only door. He then walked up and down the rows of seats and motioned for the class members to put their cellphones into the cardboard box he was carrying. Everyone did so, except for a cheeky student named Brian, who thought he was being very clever by saying that he didn't have a phone.

Mr. Fraser put down the box of cellphones and leaned down to put his freezing cold nose up against Brian's ear. Brian squeaked with fear and handed his phone to Mr. Fraser, who ate it in three bites, spitting out the glass display plate like it was a bone. He then walked to the chalkboard and wrote:

In 200 words diskribe 2 me
What the stooDent beside
yoo Would Taste Like.
Yoo hAv Ten Minutz.

Mr. Fraser leaned on the edge of his desk and remained very still while his students began their in-class essays. To their credit, the students put a good deal of thought and effort into them.

For example, Krista described her friend Brody, to her right:

"I don't think Brody would taste very good. She hardly eats anything, so I don't know how she manages to keep what meat on her she actually has. Like yesterday she ate five dried cranberries and a can of diet soda that I'm convinced she threw up afterwards. So if you ate Brody, she'd mostly be bones. I suppose you could put her into a pot and boil her for a few hours to make gravy, but it'd taste funny because she uses this stinky new hair product she got a sample of at the mall from this salesman guy who probably didn't even realize her hair is fifty percent hair extensions."

Young Kyle wrote the following words about Pablo, to his left:

"*I suppose that if I were stranded in the Andes and had to eat one of the people in the room, it'd have to be Pablo. The guy eats and eats and eats, and it really shows. I mean, he's got a muffin top on his wrists above his watch, so don't tell me he wouldn't make a kickass barbecue. He's also really slow on his feet, so if you had to chase him, he'd pretty much be yours. But it'd be easier to put a bag of chips in the middle of a rope lasso and snag him that way. He has no free will with food. Punchline? He thinks that if he goes to the gym twice a week his stomach's going to look cut. As if.*"

Young Caitlyn wrote about Steve, to her left:

"I think with Steve the issue isn't quantity so much as quality. At first glance you'd think Pablo is the best candidate, but then you have to look at what he actually eats, which is chemicals, chemicals, chemicals. He's got so many preservatives in him that he could easily be a member of the walking dead. (Not that there's anything wrong with being a member of the walking dead.) But for a more gourmet experience, you'd have to be choosier. Steve's grandparents are hippies, and some of it stuck with his parents, so in general Steve doesn't eat as much junk as everyone else does. On the down side, he has zero body fat, which means washboard abs, but also zilch in the tastiness department."

Jason wrote this about Cleo:

"It depends what you're looking for in a human. If you want grease and have no regard for your own body, throw Pablo onto the roasting spit and you're done. Be sure and bring ten gallons of barbecue sauce, and after you're sated, you can leave him on the spit and the seagulls will take care of the remains. I'd choose . . . Cleo. She's not a jock (no tough fibres; much more tender) and she doesn't buy junk food from the vending machines.

"I also don't think she's on any meds or anything. I don't know if meds would change the flavour of a person, but my uncle's a chef, and he says it's the details that make for a dining experience. Oh—she also has a stable home life, so she wouldn't taste like fear."

Mr. Fraser grunted and got up. He walked the aisles, collecting everyone's essays, then returned to his desk, where he began reading the essays as though they together comprised a menu. He lingered over them, rubbing his chin, as though trying to choose between items in a restaurant.

Finally, he held up Kyle's essay about Pablo. He gave a hoot of approval and everyone cheered.

"*Yayyyyyyyyyyy!*"

Mr. Fraser then went to the door, removed the desk and ushered them all out, save Pablo. They asked if they could have slips to allow them to roam the halls between classes, but Mr. Fraser just snarled, so they didn't push their luck or ask if they could get their phones back. He closed the door, and students in the hallway had one final glimpse of him, removing salt and pepper shakers from his shirt pocket.

about the author

DOUGLAS COUPLAND was born on a Canadian NATO base in Germany. He is the author of *Generation A, JPod*, and eleven other novels, along with non-fiction works including a recent biography of Marshall McLuhan. His books have been translated into thirty-five languages and published in most countries around the world. He is also a visual artist, sculptor, furniture designer, playwright, and screenwriter. He lives and works in Vancouver.

about the illustrator

GRAHAM ROUMIEU is the creator of the faux Bigfoot autobiography books *In Me Own Words, Me Write Book* and *I Not Dead*; as well as some non-Bigfoot related books such as *Cat & Gnome* and *101 Ways To Kill Your Boss*. Since starting work in 2001 his illustrations have appeared in the *New York Times*, the *Atlantic*, the *Guardian*, *Men's Health*, and many other places for advertising, editorial, character design and book applications.

→ CISTA · DOLOR ←